GEMSTONES
OF THE
WORLD

T&J

This edition published 2012.

Published by
TAJ BOOKS INTERNATIONAL LLP
27 Ferndown Gardens
Cobham
Surrey
KT11 2BH
UK
www.tajbooks.com

Jewelry creations on pages
28,29,35,37 top,38 right,39,41,44 right,47,57,59,63,66 right,71,
73(with A. Minton),75,77,78,79,95
courtesy of oceanbeadery.com.

All notations of errors or omissions (author inquiries, permissions) concerning the content of
this book should be addressed to info@tajbooks.com.

ISBN: 978-1-84406-198-3

Printed in China.
1 2 3 4 5 16 15 14 13 12

GEMSTONES
OF THE
WORLD

BY ELISABETH LAWS

Gemstones mark the meeting place of the human and natural worlds. Often far older than the human species (mineral gemstones, such as diamond, are formed of crystals between 1 and 3.5 billion years old), gemstones' power lies in the wonder their qualities of beauty, rarity, and durability provoke in humanity. Imbued with religious and supernatural significance, they have been a source of fascination for humankind since the earliest ages. They are worn as adornment, exchanged as valuable commodities, and regarded as purveyors of health, good fortune, and status. Any story we tell of human development—be it of religion, art, culture, trade, commerce, or the rise of scientific knowledge—will inevitably touch, at some point, on humanity's relationship with gems.

The paths of the most precious gemstones—diamond, ruby, emerald, and sapphire—have followed that of the ancient Silk Route. Commerce in precious gems paralleled the development and growth of global commerce. Jean-Baptiste Tavernier's *Six Voyages*, published in 1676, is as much a social document of travel and trade in the seventeenth century as a memoir of his occupation as a dealer in precious gems.

The diamond glittering in a modern engagement ring draws on technologies and precise cutting techniques developed over centuries. Its symmetry was facilitated by the development of the mechanized lathe and the use of diamond dust by cutters such as Louis de Berquen in the fifteenth century. Its "fire" is the result of intellectual breakthroughs such as the science of optics developed by Isaac Newton (1643–1727) and the mathematical analysis of intellectual and diamond-cutter Marcel Tolkowsky

(1899–1991). Moreover, while rolling stones may gather no moss, gemstones do gather myth and stories to them, with the famous gems traveling through history much as characters in their own right.

As long ago as 3,000–2,000 years BC, the Sumerians, who developed the first known civilization in the world, wore amulets of lapis lazuli, chalcedony, agate, and other gem materials that they considered precious, strung on thongs about their bodies. These stones were supposed to act as a conduit for the supernatural forces believed to have power over the material world. The Sumerians believed that gems gave the wearer protection in matters of childbirth, general health, wealth, battle, and relationships. The gemstones were also carved into cylindrical shapes, engraved with religious stories and hymns to particular deities, and used as seals for which they functioned as a signature when pressed onto the clay tablets that served as legal documents.

Much of what we know about the earliest ages of human civilization has come to us through artifacts that can be classified as gems of some kind. Early human history and culture is inscribed on these enigmatic artifacts, sometimes literally. In addition to the use of precious stones as talismanic adornment, the Sumerians carved their beliefs, laws, and stories of everyday life into tablets of gemstones, leaving a record of their civilization engraved upon the materials they most cherished. Their treasured status, and the imperishable quality for which they were often first valued, have ensured these gems' survival long after the cultures of which they tell have perished. Worked beads of amber, believed to be between 9,000 and 11,000 years old, have been recovered from Gough's Cave in southern England.

The relationship between humanity and its gem materials is so intimate and of such long standing that we often forget that the definition of a gemstone is, in fact, a cultural one. While the natural properties of precious stones and substances may be remarkable in themselves, their value as gemstones lies in the realm of human culture. While the refractive thermoconductive properties of ruby, as a mineral, are of scientific interest (and lent themselves to the creation of the first laser), it is only when the ruby is polished and cut that it becomes a gemstone.

The word "gem" carries with it a sense of something that has been fashioned, worked, and acculturated. Many of the qualities that humankind holds in high regard, such as the luster and fire of the crystal gems, are either not apparent in the stone's natural state or require enhancement. So while gemstones speak of humanity's awed appreciation of the natural world, they also tell us something of the roots of humankind's cultural desire to transform, embellish, and leave a trace upon the natural world.

Often a gem's value can be reckoned in monetary terms, and it can be extremely high. The classification and definition of gemstones draws on two domains: the market and science. The expertise of a certified gemologist employs a highly developed language and set of criteria to assess and grade gemstones, essentially with a view to determining commercial value. The gemologist also draws on the resources of science to assess the natural properties of gems in order to appraise them.

The modern jewelry trade has developed the mnemonic "the four Cs" in order to aid with the criteria by which gemstones are graded. The four Cs stand for color, cut, clarity, and carat. Carat is the weight of the gem. Clarity refers to the presence, or absence, of inclusions (an internal flaw, including the presence of another crystal) within a crystal. Some gemstones, such as emerald and ruby, do not occur without the presence of small traces of foreign mineral elements, or flaws. With such flaws, clarity is judged by what is visible to the naked eye.

A number of technical terms are used to describe color. Hue is the color of the gem as it first strikes the eye. Saturation is the intensity of the color and is described as ranging from dull to vivid. Tone is the lightness or darkness of the color. In addition to these characteristics, the diamond trade uses an alphabetical system to refer with precision to the color of its stones.

The color of a stone is by far the most valuable of the properties of a modern gemstone and can be enhanced or inhibited by the cut. Cutting and polishing turns a stone into jewelry and enhances the stone by maximizing the reflected light, thus creating sparkle; the Cutting Gemstones section discusses this topic in more detail.

Classifying a gemstone is complex and based on a number of relative evaluations. While it may be the case to speak of "precious" and "semi-precious" stones in the vernacular, this term lacks validity in the gem trade. Diamond, ruby, emerald, and sapphire are, however, known as the cardinal gemstones. Jade, for example, though regarded as semi-precious in the West, has long been a precious gem of cultures such as China.

The fortunes of precious gems rise and fall. Lapis lazuli was the esteemed gemstone of the ancients (as can be verified by anyone familiar with the sarcophagus of Tutankhamen), but no longer exerts this power in the modern world. Amethyst was considered precious as recently as the Victorian period until the discovery of large quantities of the mineral in Brazil caused its value to fall.

The properties for which a gemstone is prized are also subject to fashion. The diamonds of India in the nineteenth century were esteemed for their carat and were fashioned to display a more lustrous quality than the stones of today. The extraordinary optical displays of brilliance (the delivery of white light to the eye), dispersion (the splitting of white light into the colors of the spectrum), and scintillation (the reflection of light within the gem), which we value today, are of relatively recent provenance. Indeed, as early as the seventeenth century, Jean-Baptiste Tavernier recounted the tale of an unfortunate Venetian diamond cutter who introduced the fashion of faceting diamonds into a Shah's court. The rose cut he imposed on the Moghul diamond reduced its carat from 787.5 to 280 to its owner's great displeasure. The diamond cutter was fined and left penniless for his efforts.

From the times of antiquity through the Classical, Neo-Platonic, and Middle Ages, and into the modern age with its fascination for the healing properties of crystals, gemstones have been valued as a somewhat magical medicine for the body and soul. Indeed, the modern term for a gem cutter, *lapidary*, is derived from the medieval books assembled by those who assessed the medical properties of gems.

To find a more objective reckoning of the qualities and properties of gemstones, we must turn to science. One means by which gem materials can be classified, and thus assessed, is by the origin of the substance from which they are made: mineral, animal, or flora. The majority of modern gemstones are minerals, though some rocks (aggregate minerals) and biological substances are also included in the classification.

Best known of the animal-derived gemstones are pearl, coral, ivory, and tortoiseshell. Pearls are formed inside the soft tissues of sea mussels (particularly the conch) when the polyp exudes a nacreous substance (calcium carbonate) to protect itself from damage or foreign objects. The pearl forms and grows around the damaged area or object in concentric layers. The most valuable shape is a perfect, lustrous sphere, although other shapes are possible and are sold as baroque pearls.

Coral, in gemology, is the substance (calcium carbonate) secreted by marine polyps to form an exoskeleton, which becomes the reefs found in tropical oceans. Ivory is the dentine of the teeth as well as the tusks of animals such as the elephant, rhinocerous, and even the mammoth. Tortoiseshell is the polished shell of the hawksbill turtle. The trade in ivory and tortoiseshell is limited today due to concern for the species from which they are derived.

Organic gem materials not derived from animals include amber and jet. Both are the remains of ancient, coniferous trees. Amber is tree resin that has been transformed into a moderately hard stone of resinous-to-waxy luster by long processes of fossilization. Jet is the wood of the tree. Most of the ambers in existence today are the remains of a vast, prehistoric forest covering modern Norway, Sweden, Finland, and Eastern Russia and range in age from less than 1 million to more than 300 million years old. Their density is less than that of a saline solution and they can be found floating along the coastline or washed up on the shores of the Baltic Sea. Amber is also found on the coastline of Hispaniola.

Many of the mineral-based gemstones are crystal in structure. A crystal is a solid material whose atoms, molecules, or ions are formed in an orderly, repeating pattern. Minerals were formed in the earliest ages of the earth's history, in the hot mantle beneath the earth's crust. The conditions that produced the crystal gems, such as diamond, ruby, emerald, and sapphire, were the extraordinary temperatures and pressures of the cooling earth. These occasionally produced unusual bonds between the atoms of otherwise common elements, producing the relatively scarce crystal combinations of common elements that form the most precious stones.

Diamond, for example, is a form of carbon. Carbon is most commonly found as graphite (coal or pencil lead). Early conditions in the earth's mantle resulted, however, in unusual atomic bonds, creating an octahedral crystal, or diamond, rather than the usual series of layered lattices that form graphite. While the lead of a modern pencil and the Koh-i-noor diamond are chemically identical, the qualities conferred by the differing structures of their elements are radically different. The loose bonds between the molecular layers in graphite produce a soft, dull material ideal for marking paper. The structure of a diamond produces an object of adamantine hardness and dazzling optical effects.

Crystalline minerals were formed far below the earth's surface and volcanic reactions within the earth carried them upward to the earth's surface, with erosion washing them to the beds of ancient rivers or close enough to the surface to be mined. Diamonds formed as crystals deep below the earth's surface at depths of 85–120 miles. The diamond now being mined has been carried upward to the earth's surface in magma—a mixture of molten rock, volatiles, and solids existing in the high temperatures below the earth's surface—that cooled into igneous rocks such as kimberlite. Diamonds are now found mainly in host rock formations, known as kimberlite pipes, in areas of ancient geotectonic activity, such as South Africa and Brazil.

Mineral gemstones are recovered in several ways. Those that have surfaced through the erosion effects of water may be sieved for in river beds. Opal may still be recovered this way by amateurs in Australia, provided they have the proper license from Australian authorities. Other gemstones are drilled for and separated from their host rocks by a manner of sieving, because their density is often greater than the surrounding sediment. While mining is now a high-tech, professional operation in areas such as South Africa (with workers being carefully watched to prevent theft), in areas such as Myanmar (formerly, Burma), mining remains a much smaller operation and much more labor intensive, where miners dig in large, surface mines.

While gem-quality minerals may, in theory, be found anywhere, in fact, they surface only in sufficient quantities to make mining a viable operation in certain geographical locations such as Brazil, South Africa, Afghanistan, and Myanmar.

The Minerals That Produce Gemstones

Of the 2,000 or so minerals that have been identified, only 90 have produced a variety that can be recognized as being of gem quality, and of these only roughly 20 are seriously regarded as gemstones. The minerals that produce gemstones are grouped in order of species (defined by chemical and crystal structure, where relevant) and these groupings are further subdivided into varieties. Species may also be gathered into groups that share closely related properties. So, for example, garnet is a group that includes minerals with the same crystal structure, but a differing chemical composition, while ruby and sapphire are varieties of the species corundum (aluminium oxide).

Minerals are also classed according to composition and may range from being constituted of a single element to being highly complex silicates. Diamond, for example, is a form of one element (carbon). Ruby, sapphire, spinel, and zirconia are examples of the oxide class because they are aluminium oxide crystals. Turquoise and apatite are phosphates. Other mineral classes are the sulphate, halide, sulphide, and silicate classes.

Silicates can be further subdivided into groups such as inosilicates, nesosilicates, phyllosilicates, sorosilicates (such as tanzanite), tectosilicates (such as agate, amethyst, moonstone, chalcedony, onyx, and quartz), and cyclosilicates, such as tourmaline and beryl. Beryl is itself a group including emerald and aquamarine.

Much of the criteria developed in gemology to describe a gemstone's properties and optical qualities—such as chemical composition, crystal structure, refractive index, durability, specific gravity, luster, and color—refer mostly to the crystalline mineral gemstones. These are scientific terms, supplemented with technical terms to describe a stone's appearance. Chemical composition denotes the elements of which a stone is constituted. Gems may also be classified according to their crystal structure.

Gems may form single, discrete crystals (diamond is a good example) or crystocryptalline masses (collections of microscopic crystals, such as chalcedony) or amorphous masses, which are noncrystalline, such as opal. Large crystals were typically formed in areas of slow-cooling rocks, and smaller crystals were typically formed in areas of rapid-cooling rocks.

There are several classes of crystal structure, based on the symmetry of the resulting crystals. Gemstones in the cubic, or isomorphic, system include diamond, garnet, pyrite, and spinel. Gemstones in the hexagonal system include beryl, corundum, quartz, and tourmaline. Two further subdivisions of the hexagonal system are the trigonal (corundum) and rhombohedral (quartz). The tetragonal system includes gems such as zircon, rutile, and quartz. Topaz falls within the orthorhombic system. Crystals within the monoclinic system include jadeite and nephrite. Minerals whose crystals are grouped within the triclinic system include labradorite and microcline feldspar.

The refractive index of a gem is a measure of the degree to which light waves change velocity (speed) and thus direction within the stone. Durability refers to the toughness (resistance to breakage) and hardness (resistance to scratching or piercing) of a stone. Hardness is measured using the Mohs' Index. This is a nonregular scale, developed by Frierich Mohs in 1812 and reads from 1 to 10. A stone's position on this scale is relative and tells the reader that the stone will scratch the stones positioned below it and will, in turn, be marked by the stones positioned above it. Talc, for example, is given a hardness of 1, while diamond is marked as 10.

The specific gravity of a stone is a measure of its weight relative to an equivalent body of displaced water of the same shape and size. The luster of a gemstone refers to the appearance of the interaction of light waves with the surface of the stone. A technical language is employed to describe the various effects such as "earthy," "waxy," "silky," and "vitreous."

Because so much of the allure of gemstones derives from their appearance, those who are interested in gemstones must understand something of the science of light. Ordinary daylight, or "white" light, consists of a number of wavelengths, not all of which are visible to the eye. As these waves pass from the air into another medium, the velocity at which the various waves travel is altered. Depending on the chemical composition of a gemstone and its structure, some waves may be absorbed and others refracted, giving rise to the color, luster, and sparkle of a stone. In addition to these traits, gemstones can display a range of other optical phenomena.

Chatoyancy, the appearance of a ray of light streaking the stone like a cat's eye, may occur when inclusions cause a differing refraction within the stone. Asterism, the appearance of a star seeming to swim below and across the surface of the stone, is a similar optical phenomenon. Other optical effects are those of pleochromism (when a crystal has a double refractive index, causing it to change color as it is rotated), fluorescence, luminescence, and radiation. Radiation is when a stone emits absorbed light waves in a frequency other than those normally visible.

The color of a gemstone can be idiochromatic (resulting from properties of the mineral and structural composition of the stone) or allochromatic (when color is created from impurities). Diamond, for example, is colorless in its pure state, though small amounts of nitrogen substituting for carbon in the crystal lattice may give a yellow to brown hue. The fabled diamonds of the Golconda region of India contained almost negligible quantities of nitrogen, giving them a bluish haze. The term "Golconda" is used even now to refer to diamonds of this quality—fewer than one percent of those in the world. "Fancy diamonds" are the colored diamonds produced by the presence of trace elements other than carbon. The presence of boron can produce blue diamond. Radiation exposure is responsible for those of a green coloration, and irregular growth patterns within the crystal may give rise to a pink to red color. Red diamonds are extremely rare and there are only 20 known to be in existence.

Ruby and sapphire are both of the corundum species. The red coloration of ruby is usually caused by the presence of chromium. The most valuable rubies are so-called pigeon's blood rubies, associated with the Mogok Tract region of Myanmar; the adjective Myanmar now refers to a ruby of this quality from any region. The Pigeon's blood, or Myanmar, ruby has secondary hues of orange, pink, purple, and violet, which may diminish the intensity of the color. As a result, rubies are sometimes heat treated to improve color and remove inclusions, such as rutile.

Sapphire ranges in color. The presence of chromium absorbs green-yellow light waves, giving rise to a red-colored gemstone that is classed as ruby, although pink-to-orange sapphires are known as padparadscha (lotus blossom). Vanadium produces purple stones, titanium gives rise to colorless gems, iron gives sapphire a yellow to green coloration, and titanium and iron produce sapphires of the prized deep-blue coloration.

The green coloration of emerald is produced by beryllium, chromium, and vanadium. The medium to dark-toned stone is known as an emerald, while light green stones are classed as beryl.

CUTTING GEMSTONES

The properties of hue, saturation, and tone may vary depending on the direction from which a gem is viewed, and it is the job of the gem cutter to select the angle from which a gem's deepest saturation is visible, along with its greatest brilliance, and shape the stone accordingly. Similarly, effects such as pleochromism and asterism will be lost or diminished if the right cut is not selected.

Historically, gemstones were polished or cut merely to enhance their natural characteristics. Polishing a stone increases its luster. In stones other than diamond, polishing causes the surface molecules of the crystal to flow and light to play across its surface. The cabochon cut, being a raised semicircle with a level, or perhaps concave, base was the most common type of cut in antiquity. The cabochon is still used today, primarily for nontransparent gemstones and for those gems displaying phenomena such as chatoyancy and asterism. In addition, inscribing the stone or engraving it with an image, known as the process of intaglio, can be found in early periods as well as in Classical Rome.

The contemporary value of a diamond is based to a great extent upon the refractive and reflective properties of crystals: "fire" is what the majority of diamond purchasers now look for. The achievement of this particular optical effect relies on a very precise science, and the modern brilliant cut—for which Marcel Tolkowsky's 1919 publication *Diamond Design* is largely credited—was developed to enhance this effect.

The modern brilliant is cut with three main features: a crown (the top of the gem), a pavilion (the lower part), and a girdle (the wide area around the middle). In addition, it is cut with a table (the flat area on the apex of the crown), a number of polished facets (typically 33 above the girdle and 25 below), and may have a culet (a small facet at the base). In an ideal cut stone, the depth of the crown should be one-third of the total depth. For the maximum brilliance of a gem to be achieved, the greatest portion of light must fall on the front of the stone. To accomplish this, light should strike the rear facets at angles greater than the critical angle—the angle at which light is returned and which varies according to the material—of the mineral. Thus, the facets must be cut at angles greater than the critical angle, which ensures that light is totally reflected back into the eye of the observer.

To achieve a diamond's maximum brilliance, it must be cut to a very precise shape. A diamond can lose 50–60% of its (natural) carat in cutting. In order to lose as little of the gemstone as possible, a large natural stone may be cut to produce two smaller diamonds, with the wastage used as diamond dust for industrial and gem-cutting purposes.

There are a number of other significant cuts for gemstones, including the rose cut, standard round brilliant, marquise, pendeloque, emerald cut, briolette, cameo cut, and a number of fancy-cut variations.

Probably the most famous diamond cutter working today is Gabi Tolkowsky (b. 1939), great nephew of Marcel Tolkowsky. Gabi Tolkowsky introduced a number of new cuts in 1988 that are named after flowers and distinctive for their achievement of optimal brilliance, with little wastage of the natural stone. Tolkowsky is also renowned for having cut several distinctive modern diamonds, including the De Beers Centenary Diamond (273.85 carats) and the largest faceted diamond in the world, the Golden Jubilee Diamond (545.67 carats).

Gabi Tolkowsky is just one of the hundreds of thousands, if not millions of people, who have been fascinated by gemstones throughout the history of the world. The allure of gemstones will surely continue for many generations to come.

VALUABLE JEWELRY

DIAMOND BIKINI BY SUSAN ROSEN AND STEINMETZ – $30 MILLION

The diamond bikini, created by Susan Rosen with Steinmetz Diamonds, has more then 150 carats of D Flawless diamonds. The item is at the same time the most expensive diamond jewelry and the most expensive bathing suit in the world.

WHITE DIAMOND BY SOTHEBY'S – $23 MILLION.

The white diamond orignially belonged to the Sotheby's auction house and was 100.1 carat. It initially sold for $16 million but the current value is close to $23million.

DIAMOND DROP EARRINGS BY HOUSE OF HARRY WINSTON– $8.5 MILLION

These diamond drop earrings are the creation of Harry Winston. The 60 carat diamonds are mounted in platinum.

HEART-SHAPED BURMA RUBY NECKLACE – $14 MILLION

This heart-shaped ruby necklace has as a centerpiece a 40.63 carat Burma ruby and belongs to an English jeweler. It is mounted also with 155 carats worth of diamonds.

BLUE DIAMOND BY SOTHEBY'S – $7.98 MILLION

The Sotheby's blue diamond has 6.04 carats and is mounted in a superb ring that was sold in a Hong Kong exhibition at the amazing price of $7.98 million.

VALUABLE JEWELRY

DIAMOND AND EMERALD NECKLACE BY CHOPARD – $3 MILLION

This exquisite diamond and emerald necklace by Chopard was created with 191 carats of Colombian emeralds. The price is believed to be around $3 million.

DIAMOND PENDANT BY TIFFANY & CO. – $2.5 MILLION

The Tiffany diamond pendant is a simple but impeccably cut precious pear-shaped diamond. The fitting is barely noticeable, thus accentuating the beauty of the 41.4 carat diamond.

DIAMOND NECKLACE BY WILLIAM GOLDBERG – $2 MILLION.

The William Goldberg diamond necklace is a multi-hued necklace designed with many fancy-colored diamonds. The fancy diamonds on the necklace total 45 carats.

FANCY DEEP BLUE DIAMOND RING BY GRAFF – AROUND $2 MILLION

The centerpiece of this Graff diamond ring is an alluring and rare deep-blue diamond. It's cut is a clear emerald cut and its wieght is 2.4 carats.

FANCY PINK AND WHITE DIAMOND NECKLACE BY LEVIEV – CLOSE TO $2 MILLION

The Leviev diamond necklace is made of white and pink diamonds totaling 97.9 carats that are cut in a round or pear shape. It took more than a year to create this beautiful collar.

VALUABLE JEWELRY

THE CROWN JEWELS – UNITED KINGDOM

The Imperial State Crown is 31.5cm high, weighs 0.91kg, and is set with over 3,000 precious stones, including the 317 carat Cullinan II diamond.

St. Edward's Crown was refurbished from an old crown for Charles II's coronation. The gold may have come from Edward the Confessor's crown.

Made from unmarked gold and set with over 600 precious stones and pearls, the Sovereign's Orb weighs 1.32kg. It was made for Charles II's coronation in 1661.

The sceptre contains the Cullinan I diamond. At just over 530 carats, Cullinan I is the largest top-quality cut diamond in the world.

The Koh-i-Noor diamond is the largest stone in the crown worn by Queen Elizabeth The Queen Mother. Koh-i-Noor means Mountain of light.

CROWN JEWELS OF BAVARIA

The Bavarian Coronation Set consists of the Crown of Bavaria, the Crown of the Queen (originally made for Maximilian's Queen, Caroline Frederika of Baden), the State Sword, the Royal Orb, and the Royal Scepter.

SERBIAN CROWN JEWELS *Karađorđević Crown, Royal orb and scepter, and Royal Mantle buckle.*

VALUABLE JEWELRY

IMPERIAL TREASURY, VIENNA AUSTRIA

The Imperial crown, scepter, and globus cruciger. A cruciger is an orb topped by a cross, a Christian symbol of authority.

HENRIETTE DE L'ESPINE, S.A.S. LA PRINCESSE LOUIS DE CROŸ

This is a very fine pink topaz and diamond bracelet, which sold for 181,000 Swiss francs ($172,442). It was made around 1830.

THE DUCHESS OF WINDSOR'S SAPPHIRE PENDANT

This 206.82 carat sapphire pendant was created by Cartier in 1951. Expected to sell for 1.1 to 1.5 million Swiss francs, the owner ultimately withdrew it from sale for sentimental reasons.

EMPRESS EUGÉNIE'S BROOCH

This sensational antique 141 carat diamond bow brooch was made in 1855 by the Parisian jeweler François Kramer for Empress Eugénie. A Spanish countess, Eugénie de Montijo (Doña María Eugénia de Guzmán Portocarrero, Countess of Tèba) was born in Granada, Spain, in 1826, and married Louis Napoléon in 1853 at Notre Dame Cathedral. The large and impressive diamond bow was originally intended as a buckle for a diamond belt. Eugénie later asked one of her jewelers to make it more elaborate, and five diamond pampilles and a pair of diamond tassels were added. The brooch was acquired for Mrs. William B. Astor, the undisputed queen of American society. Later, Christie's sold the brooch, with an estimated value of $6 million, on behalf of its owner to the Louvre in a private sale.

VALUABLE JEWELRY

DIAMOND CORSAGE ORNAMENT

This piece, signed by Vever, circa 1900, has remained in the same family collection for a century and is one of the most important pieces of French Belle Époque jewelry to come to the market in many years. It sold for 777,000 Swiss francs ($740,263). Designed as an articulated floral branch, it is set with cushion-shaped circular and rose cut diamonds. The flower heads are set en tremblant and are mounted in silver, yellow, and pink gold. The brooch is from the Estate of Henriette de l'Espine, S.A.S. la Princesse Louis de Croÿ.

Agate

GENERAL
Category	Quartz variety
Chemical formula	SiO_2 silicon dioxide

IDENTIFICATION
Color	White to grey, light blue, orange to red, black banded
Crystal habit	Cryptocrystalline silica
Crystal system	Rhombohedral Microcrystalline
Cleavage	None
Fracture	Conchoidal with very sharp edges
Mohs scale hardness	6.5–7
Luster	Waxy
Streak	White
Diaphaneity	Translucent
Specific gravity	2.58–2.64
Refractive index	1.530–1.540
Birefringence	Up to +0.004 (B-G)
Pleochroism	Absent

Alexandrite

GENERAL

Category	Oxide minerals - Spinel group
Chemical formula	$BeAl_2O_4$
Strunz classification	04.BA.05
Crystal symmetry	Orthorhombic 2/m2/m2/m dipyramidal
Unit cell	a = 5.481 Å, b = 9.415 Å, c = 4.428 Å; Z = 8

IDENTIFICATION

Color	Various shades of green, yellow, brownish to greenish black, may be raspberry-red under incandescent light when chromian; colorless, pale shades of yellow, green, or red in transmitted light
Crystal habit	Crystals tabular or short prismatic, prominently striated
Crystal system	Orthorhombic
Twinning	Contact and penetration twins common, often repeated forming rosette structures
Cleavage	Distinct on (110), imperfect on (010), poor on {001}
Fracture	Conchoidal to uneven
Tenacity	Brittle
Mohs scale hardness	8.5
Luster	Vitreous
Streak	White
Specific gravity	3.5–3.84
Optical properties	Biaxial (+)
Refractive index	$n\alpha = 1.745$ $n\beta = 1.748$ $n\gamma = 1.754$
Pleochroism	X = red; Y = yellow-orange; Z = emerald-green
2V angle	Measured: 70°

Almandine Garnet

GENERAL
Category   Nesosilicate
Chemical formula $Fe_2{+}3Al_2Si_3O_{12}$
Strunz classification   09.AD.25

IDENTIFICATION
Color   Reddish orange to red, slightly purplish red to reddish purple, usually dark in tone
Cleavage   None
Fracture   Conchoidal
Mohs scale hardness   7–7.5
Luster   Greasy to vitreous
Specific gravity   4.05 (+.25, –0.12)
Polish luster   Vitreous to subadamantine
Optical properties   Single refractive, and often anomalous double refractive
Refractive index   1.790 (+/– 0.030)
Birefringence   None
Pleochroism   None
Dispersion   0.024
Ultraviolet fluorescence   Inert
Absorption spectra   Usually at 504, 520, and 573nm, may also have faint lines at 423, 460, 610 and 680-690nm

Amber

Amber is fossilized tree resin (not sap), which has been appreciated for its color and natural beauty since Neolithic times. Amber is used as an ingredient in perfumes, as a healing agent in folk medicine, and as jewelry. There are five classes of amber, defined on the basis of their chemical constituents. Because amber originates as a soft, sticky tree resin, it sometimes contains animal and plant material as inclusions. Amber occurring in coal seams is also called resinite, and the term ambrite is applied to that found specifically within New Zealand coal seams.

Amber is heterogeneous in composition, but consists of several resinous bodies more or less soluble in alcohol, ether, and chloroform, associated with an insoluble bituminous substance. Amber is a macromolecule by free radical polymerization of several precursors in the labdane family, e.g. communic acid, cummunol, and biformene. These labdanes are diterpenes ($C_{20}H_{32}$) and trienes, equipping the organic skeleton with three alkene groups for polymerization. As amber matures over the years, more polymerization takes place as well as isomerization reactions, crosslinking, and cyclization.

The average composition of amber leads to the general formula $C_{10}H_{16}O$.

Amethyst

GENERAL

Category	Mineral variety
Chemical formula	Silica (silicon dioxide, SiO_2)

IDENTIFICATION

Color	Purple, violet
Crystal habit	6-sided prism ending in 6-sided pyramid (typical)
Crystal system	Rhombohedral class 32
Twinning	Dauphine law, Brazil law, and Japan law
Cleavage	None
Fracture	Conchoidal
Mohs scale hardness	7, lower in impure varieties
Luster	Vitreous/glossy
Streak	White
Diaphaneity	Transparent to translucent
Specific gravity	2.65 constant; variable in impure varieties
Optical properties	Uniaxial (+)
Refractive index	$n\omega$ = 1.543–1.553 $n\varepsilon$ = 1.552–1.554
Birefringence	+0.009 (B-G interval)
Pleochroism	None
Melting point	1650 ± 75 °C
Solubility	Insoluble in common solvents
Other characteristics	Piezoelectric

Aquamarine

Aquamarine is a blue or turquoise variety of beryl. Its name derives from the Latin *aqua marina*, which means "water of the sea." It occurs at most localities that yield ordinary beryl, with some of the finest coming from Russia. The gem-gravel placer deposits of Sri Lanka contain aquamarine. Clear yellow beryl, such as that occurring in Brazil, is sometimes called aquamarine chrysolite. When corundum presents the bluish tint of typical aquamarine, it is often termed Oriental aquamarine. The deep blue version of aquamarine is called maxixe.

The pale blue color of aquamarine is attributed to Fe^{2+}. When both Fe^{2+} and Fe^{3+} are present, the color is a darker blue, as in maxixe. The dark-blue maxixe color can be produced in green, pink, or yellow beryl by irradiating it with high-energy particles, such as gamma rays, neutrons or even X-rays.

In the United States, aquamarines can be found at the summit of Mt. Antero in the Sawatch Range in central Colorado. Aquamarine has also been discovered in the Big Horn Mountains, near Powder River Pass, in Wyoming. Brazil mines aquamarine in the states of Minas Gerais, Espírito Santo, and Bahia, and minimally in Rio Grande do Norte. The mines of Colombia, Zambia, Madagascar, Malawi, Tanzania, and Kenya also produce aquamarine. The largest aquamarine of gemstone quality ever mined was found in Marambaia, Minas Gerais, Brazil, in 1910. The gem weighed over 110 kg, and its dimensions were 48.5 cm (19 in) long and 42 cm (17 in) in diameter.

Aventurine

Aventurine is a form of quartz, characterized by its translucency and the presence of platy mineral inclusions that give it a shimmering or glistening effect termed aventurescence.

The most common color of aventurine is green, but it may also be orange, brown, yellow, blue, or gray. Chrome-bearing fuchsite, a variety of muscovite mica, is the classic inclusion and gives a silvery green or blue sheen to the gemstone. The colors orange and brown are attributed to hematite or goethite. Because aventurine is a rock, its physical properties vary. Its specific gravity may lie between 2.64 and 2.69, and its hardness is somewhat lower than single-crystal quartz at around 6.5.

Aventurine feldspar or sunstone can be confused with orange and red aventurine quartzite, although the former is generally of a higher transparency. Aventurine is often banded and an overabundance of fuchsite may render it opaque, in which case it may be mistaken for malachite at first glance.

Beryl

GENERAL

Category	Silicate mineral
Chemical formula	Be3Al2(SiO3)6
Crystal symmetry	(6/m 2/m 2/m) – Dihexagonal Dipyramidal
Unit cell	a = 9.21 Å, c = 9.19 Å; Z = 2

IDENTIFICATION

Molar mass	537.50
Color	Green, blue, yellow, colorless, pink and others
Crystal habit	Massive to well crystalline
Crystal system	Hexagonal (6/m 2/m 2/m), Space group: P 6/mcc
Cleavage	Imperfect on the [0001]
Fracture	Conchoidal
Mohs scale hardness	7.5–8
Luster	Vitreous
Streak	White
Diaphaneity	Transparent to opaque
Specific gravity	Average 2.76
Optical properties	Uniaxial (-)
Refractive index	$n\omega$ = 1.564–1.595, $n\varepsilon$ = 1.568–1.602
Birefringence	δ = 0.0040–0.0070

Chalcedony

General

Category	Oxide mineral
Chemical formula	Silica (silicon dioxide, SiO2)

Identification

Molar mass	60 g / mol
Color	Various
Crystal system	Trigonal, monoclinic
Cleavage	Absent
Fracture	Uneven, splintery, conchoidal
Mohs scale hardness	6–7
Luster	Waxy, vitreous, dull, greasy, silky
Streak	White
Diaphaneity	Translucent
Specific gravity	2.59–2.61

Citrine

Citrine is a variety of quartz. Its color ranges from a pale yellow to brown. Natural citrines are rare. Most commercial citrines are heat-treated amethyst. Citrine contains traces of Fe^{3+} and is rarely found naturally. The name is derived from the Latin *citrina,* which means "yellow."

Pure quartz, traditionally called rock crystal or clear quartz, is colorless and transparent or translucent. Quartz is the second most-abundant mineral in the Earth's continental crust. Feldspar is the most abundant mineral. It is made of a continuous framework of SiO_4 silicon–oxygen tetrahedra, with each oxygen shared by two tetrahedra, producing an overall formula of SiO_2. Quartz is found in many varieties, some of which are semi-precious gemstones. In Europe and the Middle East, quartz in its many varieties has historically been one of the most commonly used minerals in jewelry and hardstone carvings.

Corundum

GENERAL

Category	Oxide mineral – Hematite group
Chemical formula	Aluminium oxide, Al2O3
Strunz classification	04.CB.05
Dana classification	4.3.1.1
Crystal symmetry	Trigonal (32/m)
Unit cell	a = 4.75 Å, c = 12.982 Å; Z=6

IDENTIFICATION

Color	Colorless, gray, brown; pink to pigeon-blood-red, orange, yellow, green, blue to cornflower blue, violet; may be color zoned, asteriated mainly grey and brown
Crystal habit	Steep bipyramidal, tabular, prismatic, rhombohedral crystals, massive or granular
Crystal system	Trigonal (Hexagonal Scalenohedral)
Symbol	(32/m)
Space group:	R3c
Twinning	Polysynthetic twinning common
Cleavage	None, parting in 3 directions
Fracture	Conchoidal to uneven
Mohs scale hardness	9 (defining mineral)
Luster	Adamantine to vitreous
Streak	White
Diaphaneity	Transparent, translucent to opaque
Specific gravity	3.95–4.10
Optical properties	Uniaxial (–)
Refractive index	nω = 1.767–1.772 nε = 1.759–1.763
Pleochroism	None
Melting point	2044 °C
Alters to	May alter to mica on surfaces causing a decrease in hardness
Other characteristics	May fluoresce or phosphoresce under UV

Diamond

GENERAL

Category	Native Minerals
Chemical formula	C
Strunz classification	01.CB.10a

IDENTIFICATION

Molar mass	12.01 g·mol-1
Color	Typically yellow, brown or gray to colorless; less often blue, green, black, translucent white, pink, violet, orange, purple and red
Crystal habit	Octahedral
Crystal system	Isometric-Hexoctahedral (Cubic)
Cleavage	111 (perfect in four directions)
Fracture	Conchoidal (shell-like)
Mohs scale hardness	10
Luster	Adamantine
Diaphaneity	Transparent to subtransparent to translucent
Specific gravity	3.52 ± 0.01
Density	3.5–3.53 g/cm3
Polish luster	Adamantine
Optical properties	Isotropic
Refractive index	2.418 (at 500 nm)
Birefringence	None
Pleochroism	None
Dispersion	0.044
Melting point	Pressure dependent

Emerald

GENERAL

Category	Beryl variety
Chemical formula	Be3Al2(SiO3)6
Crystal symmetry	(6/m 2/m 2/m) – Dihexagonal Dipyramidal
Unit cell	a = 9.21 Å, c = 9.19 Å; Z = 2

IDENTIFICATION

Molar mass	537.50
Color	Green shades
Crystal habit	Massive to well crystalline
Crystal system	Hexagonal (6/m 2/m 2/m) Space group: P6/mcc
Cleavage	Imperfect on the [0001]
Fracture	Conchoidal
Mohs scale hardness	7.5–8
Luster	Vitreous
Streak	White
Diaphaneity	Transparent to opaque
Specific gravity	Average 2.76
Optical properties	Uniaxial (-)
Refractive index	$n\omega$ = 1.564–1.595,
	$n\varepsilon$ = 1.568–1.602
Birefringence	δ = 0.0040–0.0070

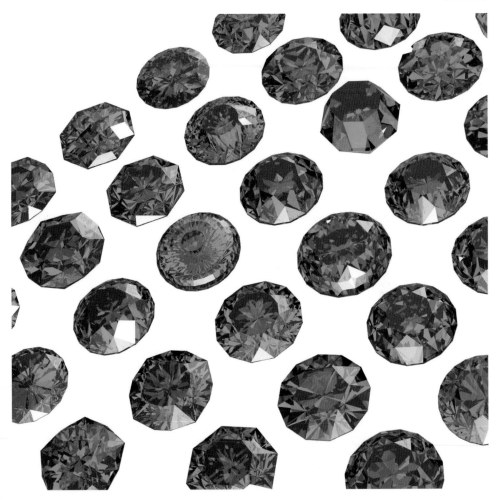

53

Fluorite

General

Category	Halide mineral
Chemical formula	CaF2
Strunz classification	03.AB.25
Crystal symmetry	Isometric H–M Symbol 4/m 3 2/m
Unit cell	a = 5.4626 Å; Z=4

Identification

Color	Colorless, white, purple, blue, green, yellow, orange, red, pink, brown, bluish black; commonly zoned
Crystal habit	Occurs as well-formed coarse sized crystals also nodular, botryoidal, rarely columnar or fibrous; granular, massive
Crystal system	Isometric, cF12, SpaceGroup Fm3m, No. 225
Twinning	Common on {111}, interpenetrant, flattened
Cleavage	Octahedral, perfect on {111}, parting on {011}
Fracture	Subconchoidal to uneven
Tenacity	Brittle
Mohs scale hardness	4 (defining mineral)
Luster	Vitreous
Streak	White
Diaphaneity	Transparent to translucent
Specific gravity	3.175–3.184; to 3.56 if high in rare-earth elements
Optical properties	Isotropic; weak anomalous anisotropism
Refractive index	1.433–1.448
Fusibility	3

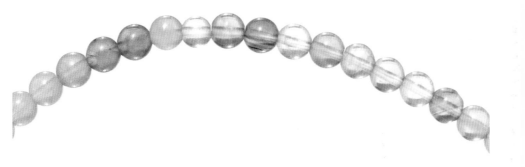

Iolite

Category	Silicate mineral
Chemical formula	$(Mg,Fe)2Al4Si5O18$
Strunz classification	09.CJ.10
Dana classification	61.02.01.01 Cordierite group
Crystal symmetry	2/m 2/m 2/m Orthorhombic - Dipyramidal
Unit cell	a = 17.079 Å, b = 9.730 Å, c = 9.356 Å; Z = 4

Color	Blue, smoky blue, bluish violet; greenish, yellowish brown, gray; colorless to very pale blue in thin section
Crystal habit	Pseudo-hexagonal prismatic twins, as imbedded grains, and massive
Crystal system	Orthorhombic - Dipyramidal Space Group: C ccm
Twinning	Common on {110}, {130}, simple, lamellar, cyclical
Cleavage	Fair on {100}, poor on {001} and {010}
Fracture	Subconchoidal
Tenacity	Brittle
Mohs scale hardness	7–7.5
Luster	Greasy or vitreous
Streak	White
Specific gravity	2.57–2.66
Optical properties	Usually optically (-), sometimes (+); 2V = 0-90°
Refractive index	$n\alpha$ = 1.527–1.560 $n\beta$ = 1.532–1.574 $n\gamma$ = 1.538–1.578; Indices increase with Fe content
Pleochroism	X = pale yellow, green; Y = violet, blue-violet; Z = pale blue
Fusibility	On thin edges

Jade

Jade is an ornamental stone. The term jade is applied to two different metamorphic rocks that are made up of different silicate minerals: nephrite and ferroactinolite.

Nephrite consists of a microcrystaline interlocking fibrous matrix of the calcium, magnesium-iron-rich amphibole mineral series tremolite (calcium-magnesium) and ferroactinolite (calcium-magnesium-iron). The middle member of this series, an intermediate composition, is called actinolite. Actinole is the silky fibrous mineral form of asbestos. The higher the iron content, the greener the color.

Jadeite is a sodium- and aluminium-rich pyroxene. The gem form of the mineral is a microcrystaline interlocking crystal matrix.

Kunzite

Kunzite is a pink- to lilac-colored gemstone, a variety of spodumene. Its color comes from minor to trace amounts of manganese. Some, but not all, kunzite used for gemstones has been heated to enhance its color.

Kunzite is also frequently irradiated to enhance its color. Many kunzites fade when exposed to sunlight. It was discovered in 1902, and was named after George Frederick Kunz, Tiffany & Co.'s chief jeweler at the time, and a noted mineralogist. The gemstibe has been found in Brazil, the US, Canada, Mexico, Sweden, Western Australia, Afghanistan, and Pakistan.

Lapis Lazuli

GENERAL

Category	Rock
Chemical formula	Mixture of minerals

IDENTIFICATION

Color	Blue, mottled with white calcite and brassy pyrite
Crystal habit	Compact, massive
Crystal system	None, lapis is a rock; lazurite, the main constituent, frequently occurs as dodecahedra
Cleavage	Uneven-Conchoidal
Mohs scale hardness	5–5.5
Luster	Dull
Streak	Light blue
Specific gravity	2.7–2.9
Refractive index	1.5
Other characteristics	The variations in composition cause a wide variation in the above values

Lapis Lazuli

Lepidolite

GENERAL

Category	Silicate mineral
Chemical formula	KLi2Al(Al,Si)3O10(F,OH)2
Strunz classification	09.EC.20
Crystal symmetry	Monoclinic H-M symbol: 2/m
Space group	C 2/m,Cm
Unit cell	a = 5.209(2) Å b = 9.011(5) Å, c = 10.149(5) Å; β = 100:77(4)°; Z = 2

IDENTIFICATION

Color	Pink, purple, rose-red, violet-gray, yellowish, white, colorless
Crystal habit	Tabular to prismatic pseudohexagonal crystals, scaly aggregates and massive
Crystal system	Monoclinic
Twinning	Rare, composition plane {001}
Cleavage	{001} perfect
Fracture	Uneven
Mohs scale hardness	2.5–3
Luster	Vitreous to pearly
Streak	White
Diaphaneity	Transparent to translucent
Specific gravity	2.8–2.9
Optical properties	Biaxial (-)
Refractive index	nα = 1.525–1.548, nβ = 1.551–1.58, nγ = 1.554–1.586
Birefringence	0.0290–0.0380
Pleochroism	X = almost colorless; Y = Z = pink, pale violet
2V angle	0°–58° measured

Malachite

GENERAL

Category	Carbonate mineral
Chemical formula	$Cu_2CO_3(OH)_2$
Strunz classification	05.BA.10

IDENTIFICATION

Molar mass	221.1 g/mol
Color	Bright green, dark green, blackish green, commonly banded in masses; green to yellowish green in transmitted light
Crystal habit	Massive, botryoidal, stalactitic; crystals are acicular to tabular prismatic
Crystal system	Monoclinic—prismatic H-M Symbol (2/m), space group P21/a
Twinning	Common as contact or penetration twins on {100} and {201}. Polysynthetic twinning also present.
Cleavage	Perfect on {201}, fair on {010}
Fracture	Subconchoidal to uneven
Mohs scale hardness	3.5–4.0
Luster	Adamantine to vitreous; silky if fibrous; dull to earthy if massive
Streak	Light green
Diaphaneity	Translucent to opaque
Specific gravity	3.6–4
Optical properties	Biaxial (–)
Refractive index	$n\alpha = 1.655$ $n\beta = 1.875$ $n\gamma = 1.909$
Birefringence	$\delta = 0.254$

Moonstone

GENERAL

Category   Feldspar variety

IDENTIFICATION

Color   Can be numerous colors, including blue, grey, white, pink, green and brown
Fracture   Uneven to conchoidal
Mohs scale hardness 6.0
Luster   Opalescent
Streak   White
Specific gravity   2.61

Onyx

GENERAL

Category	Oxide minerals - Spinel group
Chemical formula	$BeAl_2O_4$
Strunz classification	04.BA.05
Crystal symmetry	Orthorhombic 2/m2/m2/m dipyramidal
Unit cell	a = 5.481 Å, b = 9.415 Å, c = 4.428 Å; Z = 8

IDENTIFICATION

Color	Various shades of green, yellow, brownish to greenish black, may be raspberry-red under incandescent light when chromian; colorless, pale shades of yellow, green, or red in transmitted light
Crystal habit	Crystals tabular or short prismatic, prominently striated
Crystal system	Orthorhombic
Twinning	Contact and penetration twins common, often-repeated forming rosette structures
Cleavage	Distinct on (110), imperfect on (010), poor on {001}
Fracture	Conchoidal to uneven
Tenacity	Brittle
Mohs scale hardness	8.5
Luster	Vitreous
Streak	White
Specific gravity	3.5–3.84
Optical properties	Biaxial (+)
Refractive index	$n\alpha = 1.745$ $n\beta = 1.748$ $n\gamma = 1.754$
Pleochroism	X = red; Y = yellow-orange; Z = emerald-green
2V angle	Measured: 70°

Opal

GENERAL
Category   Mineraloid
Chemical formula   Hydrated silica, $SiO_2 \cdot nH_2O$

IDENTIFICATION
Color   Colorless, white, yellow, red, orange, green, brown, black, blue
Crystal habit   Irregular veins, in masses, in nodules
Crystal system   Amorphous
Fracture   Conchoidal to uneven
Mohs scale hardness   5.5–6
Luster   Subvitreous to waxy
Streak   White
Diaphaneity   Opaque, translucent, transparent
Specific gravity   2.15 (+.08, –0.90)
Density   2.09
Polish luster   Vitreous to resinous
Optical properties   Single refractive, often anomalous double refractive due to strain
Refractive index   1.450 (+.020, –0.080) Mexican opal may read as low as 1.37, but typically reads 1.42–1.43
Ultraviolet fluorescence   Black or white body color: inert to white to moderate light blue, green, or yellow in long and short wave. May also phosphoresce; common opal: inert to strong green or yellowish green in long and short wave, may phosphoresce; fire opal: inert to moderate greenish brown in long and short wave, may phosphoresce
Absorption spectra   Green stones: 660nm, 470nm cutoff
Diagnostic features   Darkening upon heating
Solubility   Hot saltwater, bases, methanol, humic acid, hydrofluoric acid

Pearl

GENERAL

Category	Mineral
Chemical formula	CaCO3

IDENTIFICATION

Color	White, pink, silver-, cream-, golden-colored, green, blue, black, yellow, rainbow
Cleavage	None
Mohs scale hardness	2.5–4.5
Streak	White
Specific gravity	2.60–2.85
Dispersion	None
Ultraviolet	Fluorescence weak, cannot be evaluated

Peridot

GENERAL

Category	Mineral
Chemical formula	(Mg, Fe)2SiO4

IDENTIFICATION

Color	Yellow to yellow-green, olive-green, to brownish, sometimes a lime-green, to emerald-ish hue
Crystal system	Orthorhombic
Cleavage	Poor
Fracture	Conchoidal
Mohs scale hardness	6.5–7
Luster	Vitreous (glassy)
Streak	White
Specific gravity	3.2–4.3
Refractive index	1.64–1.70
Birefringence	+0.036

Quartz

GENERAL

Category	Silicate mineral
Chemical formula	Silica (silicon dioxide, SiO2)
Strunz classification	04.DA.05
Dana classification	75.01.03.01
Crystal symmetry	Trigonal H–M Symbol 32
Unit cell	a = 4.9133 Å, c = 5.4053 Å; Z = 3

IDENTIFICATION

Color	From colorless to black, through various colors
Crystal system	α-quartz: trigonal trapezohedral class 3 2; β-quartz: hexagonal 622
Twinning	Common Dauphine law, Brazil law and Japan law
Cleavage	{0110} Indistinct
Fracture	Conchoidal
Tenacity	Brittle
Mohs scale hardness	7; lower in impure varieties (defining mineral)
Luster	Vitreous; waxy to dull when massive
Streak	White
Diaphaneity	Transparent to nearly opaque
Specific gravity	2.65; variable 2.59–2.63 in impure varieties
Optical properties	Uniaxial (+)
Refractive index	$n\omega$ = 1.543–1.545 $n\varepsilon$ = 1.552–1.554
Birefringence	+0.009 (B-G interval)
Melting point	1670 °C (β tridymite) 1713 °C (β cristobalite)
Solubility	Insoluble at STP; 1 ppmmass at 400 °C and 34 bar to 2600 ppmmass at 500 °C and 103 bar
Other characteristics	Piezoelectric, may be triboluminescent, chiral

Rhodochrosite

GENERAL

Category	Mineral species
Chemical formula	$MnCO_3$
Strunz classification	05.AB.05

IDENTIFICATION

Molar mass	114.95 g/mol
Color	Red to pink, brown to yellow, gray to white
Crystal habit	Massive to well crystalline
Crystal system	Trigonal - Hexagonal Scalenohedral
Twinning	On the {0112} uncommon
Cleavage	On the [1011] perfect
Fracture	Uneven, conchoidal
Tenacity	Brittle
Mohs scale hardness	3.5–4
Luster	Vitreous
Streak	White
Diaphaneity	Transparent to translucent
Specific gravity	3.5–3.7
Density	3.7 g/cm³
Optical properties	Uniaxial (−)
Birefringence	δ = 0.218
Pleochroism	Weak

Ruby

GENERAL
Category   Mineral variety
Chemical formula   Aluminium oxide with chromium, Al2O3:Cr

IDENTIFICATION
Color   Red, may be brownish, purplish or pinkish
Crystal habit   Varies with locality; terminated tabular hexagonal prisms
Crystal system   Trigonal (Hexagonal Scalenohedral), symbol (−3 2/m), space Group: R-3c
Cleavage   No true cleavage
Fracture   Uneven or conchoidal
Mohs scale hardness   9.0
Luster   Vitreous
Streak   White
Diaphaneity   Transparent
Specific gravity   4.0
Refractive index $n\omega = 1.768 – 1.772$ $n\varepsilon = 1.760 – 1.763$
Birefringence   0.008
Pleochroism   Orangey red, purplish red
Ultraviolet fluorescence   Red under longwave
Melting point   2044 °C

Saphire

GENERAL

Category	Oxide mineral
Chemical formula	Aluminium oxide, Al2O3

IDENTIFICATION

Color	Every color except for red, which is called a ruby, or pinkish-orange (the padparadscha)
Crystal habit	Massive and granular
Crystal system	Trigonal
Symbol	(32/m)
Space Group:	R3c
Cleavage	None
Fracture	Conchoidal, splintery
Mohs scale hardness	9.0
Luster	Vitreous
Streak	White
Specific gravity	3.95–4.03
Optical properties	Abbe number 72.2
Refractive index	$n\omega = 1.768–1.772$ $n\varepsilon = 1.760–1.763$
Birefringence	0.008
Pleochroism	Strong
Melting point	2030–2050 °C
Fusibility	Infusible
Solubility	Insoluble
Other characteristics	Coefficient of thermal expansion $(5.0–6.6)\times10–6/K$

Spinel

GENERAL

Category	Oxide minerals - Spinel group
Chemical formula	$MgAl_2O_4$
Strunz classification	04.BB.05

IDENTIFICATION

Color	Various, red to blue to mauve, dark green, brown, black
Crystal habit	Cubic, octahedral
Crystal system	Isometric
Cleavage	Indistinct
Fracture	Conchoidal, uneven
Mohs scale hardness	7.5–8.0
Luster	Vitreous
Streak	White
Diaphaneity	Transparent to translucent
Specific gravity	3.6–4.1
Optical properties	Isotropic
Refractive index	1.719
Pleochroism	Absent
Solubility	None
Other characteristics	Nonmagnetic, non-radioactive, sometimes fluorescent (red)

GENERAL

Category	Sorosilicate
Chemical formula	(Ca2Al3(SiO4)(Si2O7)O(OH))
Strunz classification	09.BG.10

IDENTIFICATION

Color	Purple to blue
Crystal habit	Crystals flattened in an acicular manner, may be fibrously curved
Crystal system	Orthorhombic
Cleavage	Perfect {010} imperfect {100}
Fracture	Uneven to conchoidal
Mohs scale hardness	6.5
Luster	Vitreous, pearly on cleavage surfaces
Streak	White or colorless
Specific gravity	3.10–3.38
Optical properties	Biaxial positive
Refractive index	1.69–1.70
Birefringence	0.006–0.018
Pleochroism	Present, dichroism or trichroism depending on color

Topaz

GENERAL

Category	Silicate mineral
Chemical formula	Al2SiO4(F,OH)2
Strunz classification	9.AF.35
Crystal symmetry	Orthorhombic dipyramidal
H-M symbol:	(2/m 2/m 2/m)
Space group:	Pbnm
Unit cell	a = 4.65 Å, b = 8.8 Å,c = 8.4 Å; Z = 4

IDENTIFICATION

Color	Colorless (if no impurities), blue, brown, orange, gray, yellow, green, pink and reddish pink
Crystal habit	Prismatic crystals with faces striated parallel to long dimension; also columnar, compact, massive
Crystal system	Orthorhombic
Cleavage	[001] Perfect
Fracture	Subconchoidal to uneven
Mohs scale hardness	8 (defining mineral)
Luster	Vitreous
Streak	White
Diaphaneity	Transparent
Specific gravity	3.49–3.57
Optical properties	Biaxial (+)
Refractive index	nα = 1.606–1.629 nβ = 1.609–1.631 nγ = 1.616–1.638
Birefringence	δ = 0.010
Pleochroism	Weak in thick sections X = yellow; Y = yellow, violet, reddish; Z = violet, bluish, yellow, pink
Other characteristics	Fluorescent, short UV=golden yellow, long UV=cream

Tourmaline

GENERAL

Category	Cyclosilicate
Chemical formula	(Ca,K,Na)(Al,Fe,Li,Mg,Mn)3(Al,Cr, Fe,V)6 (BO3)3(Si,Al,B)6O18(OH,F)4

IDENTIFICATION

Color	Most commonly black, but can range from brown, violet, green, pink, or in a dual-colored pink and green
Crystal habit	Parallel and elongated; acicular prisms, sometimes radiating; massive; scattered grains (in granite)
Crystal system	Trigonal
Cleavage	Indistinct
Fracture	Uneven, small conchoidal, brittle
Mohs scale hardness	7–7.5
Luster	Vitreous, sometimes resinous
Streak	White
Specific gravity	3.06 (+.20 –0.06)
Density	2.82–3.32
Polish luster	Vitreous
Optical properties	Double refractive, uniaxial negative
Refractive index	$n\omega$ = 1.635–1.675 $n\varepsilon$ = 1.610–1.650
Birefringence	–0.018 to – 0.040; typically about 0.020, but in dark stones it may reach 0.040
Pleochroism	Typically moderate to strong; Red Tourmaline: Definite, dark red,light red; Green Tourmaline: Strong, dark green, yellow-green; Brown Tourmaline: Definite;,dark brown, light brown; Blue Tourmaline: Strong; dark blue, light blue
Dispersion	0.017

Turquoise

GENERAL

Category	Phosphate minerals
Chemical formula	CuAl6(PO4)4(OH)8·4H2O
Strunz classification	08.DD.15

IDENTIFICATION

Colour	Blue, blue-green, green
Crystal habit	Massive, nodular
Crystal system	Triclinic
Cleavage	Good to perfect – usually N/A
Fracture	Conchoidal
Mohs scale hardness	5–7
Lustre	Waxy to subvitreous
Streak	Bluish white
Specific gravity	2.6–2.9
Optical properties	Biaxial (+)
Refractive index	$n\alpha$ = 1.610 $n\beta$ = 1.615 $n\gamma$ = 1.650
Birefringence	+0.040
Pleochroism	Weak
Fusibility	Fusible in heated HCl
Solubility	Soluble in HCl

INDEX